Woodland of Wonders

Beaver Builds a Wetland

Kenzie Field

In the woodland of wonders
a river runs through.
A young beaver in search
of a home – this might do.

His eyes gaze round the spot
for what trees he can chew.
Trees of pine are too sappy,
but cottonwoods will do.

With his tail out for balance,

he reaches the tree.

Using teeth of strong iron,

the branches come free.

He starts stacking the wood
one by one, it grows tall.
All together each piece
starts to build a dam wall.

The calm river gains depth
inch by inch, day by day.
As the dam slows the water,
a wetland takes way.

As the sun shines on down,
some new plants start to grow.
This new wetland has water
of blue indigo.

To enjoy his first swim
in the deep pond of blue,
using webbed flipper feet
to transport his way through.

What the beaver soon learns,
as he swims on his own.
No one else is here with him.
He feels all alone.

He will just have to wait
as he knows friends will find
this lush sanctum of greens.
It is one of a kind!

Iridescent wood ducks
soar down flying with grace,
they both land on a branch
for a rest in this space.

Plants like cattails now sprout
at the edge of the pond
and swift dragonfly legs,
with ease, grasp tightly on.

Frogs begin leaping in

and brown trout start to spawn.

When the season turns spring,
there will be baby fawns.

Chickadees, ravens, grasshoppers, and ducks.

Porcupines, owls, coyotes, and bucks.

Pelicans, turtles, woodpeckers, and minks.

Damselflies, blackbirds, kingfishers, and lynx.

Baltimore orioles, swans, and a moose.

Butterflies, cormorants, loons, and a goose.

Snowshoe hares, eagles, squirrels, and a fox.

Black spiders, herons, mosquitoes and hawks.

Nuthatches, badgers, mergansers, and bats.

Ladybugs, osprey, raccoons, and muskrats.

A new ecosystem grows
into animals' homes.
This lush wetland is now
an impressive biome.

Our strong beaver looks round
at the family he's made,
a community started
by logs he had laid.

Dedicated to
my son Beau & new baby to come

Inspired by my environmental science background,
and educating our little humans about our natural environment.

FIELD KITS Publishing

May 2024

Author

Kenzie Field

Editors

Kathryn Boucher & Jaimee Guenther

Illustrator

Canva AI

ISBN: 978-1-7383200-6-6

© All rights reserved. No part of this book may be reproduced in any form or by any electronic or mechanical means, including information storage and retrieval systems, without permission in writing from the publisher and copyright holder, except in the case of brief quotations embodied in critical articles and reviews. This is a work of creative nonfiction. Some parts have been fictionalized to varying degrees.

Woodland of Wonders Book Series

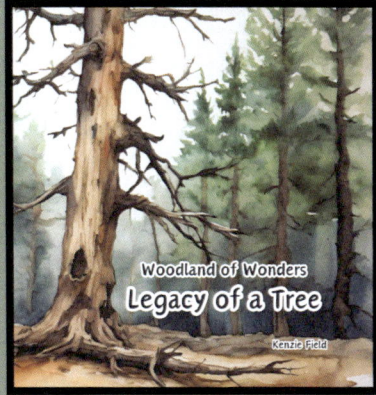

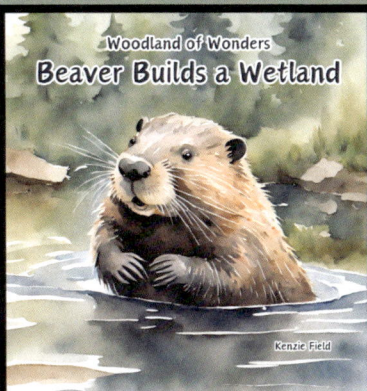

www.ingramcontent.com/pod-product-compliance
Lightning Source LLC
Chambersburg PA
CBRC091724070526
44585CB00009B/170